Pybabi.com

$e^x i\ pi$

ISBN 979-8-9875895-5-7

Published by Pybabi Publishing

This book is dedicated to my 100 year old grandmother Annie Porter who holds a special place in my heart. I love you.

One day a big storm
hit the Pybabi Village.
The rain came down
the wind blew, shook
the village through
and through.

1

PYBABI VILLAGE

2

One day a big storm hit the Pybabi Village. The rain came down the wind blew and shook the village through and through.

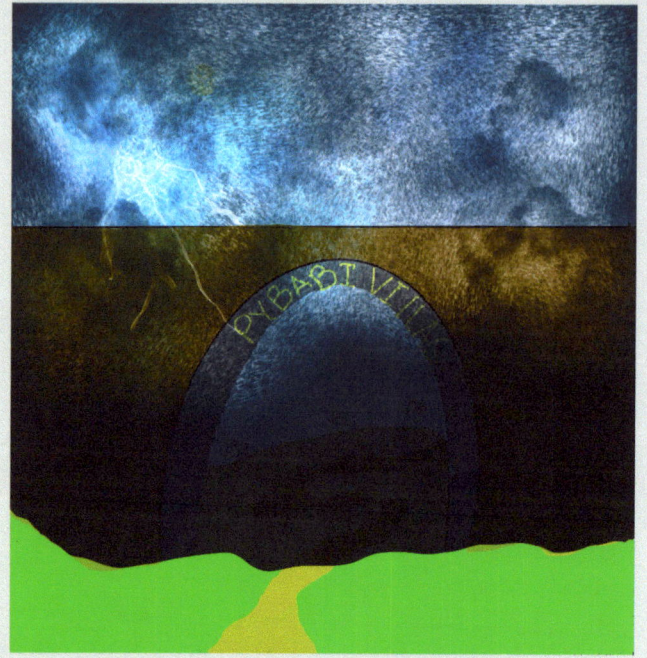

Even though the storm shook our village through and through. We want to share our thoughts with you.

We don't know what your storm could be but we hope our words can bring relief.

3

One day a big storm hit the Pybabi Village. The rain came down the wind blew and shook the village through and through.

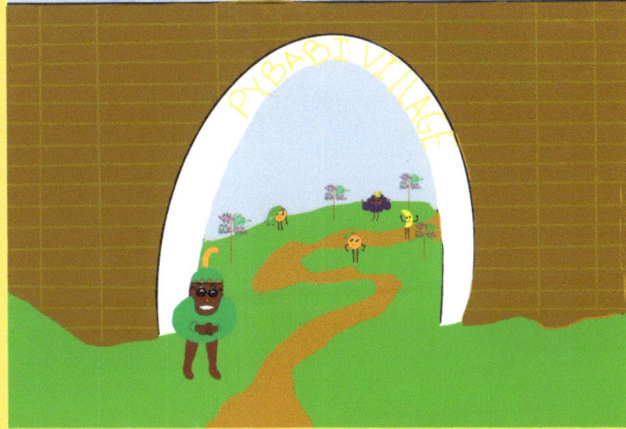

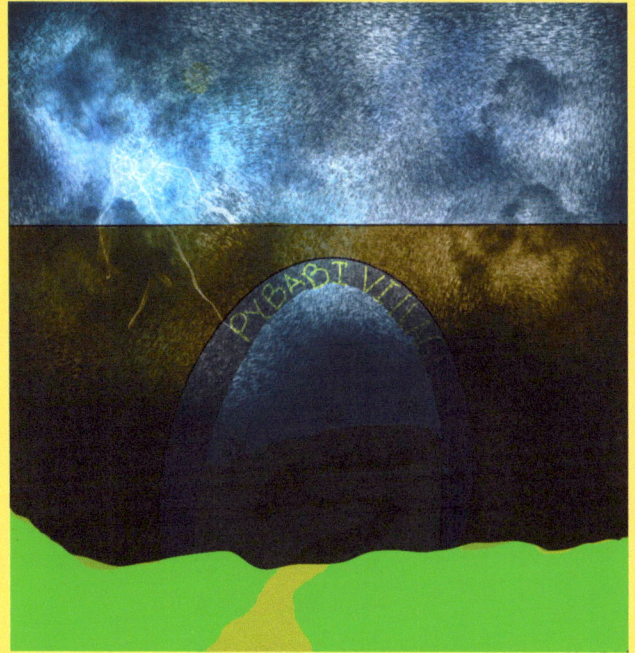

After the storm you may feel cold and blue but always remember good people will care for you!

Ogi Orange

4

One day a big storm hit the Pybabi Village. The rain came down the wind blew and shook the village through and through.

After the storm you may not feel right but please remember, a good person will hold you tight.

Mayor Pear

One day a big storm hit the Pybabi Village. The rain came down the wind blew and shook the village through and through.

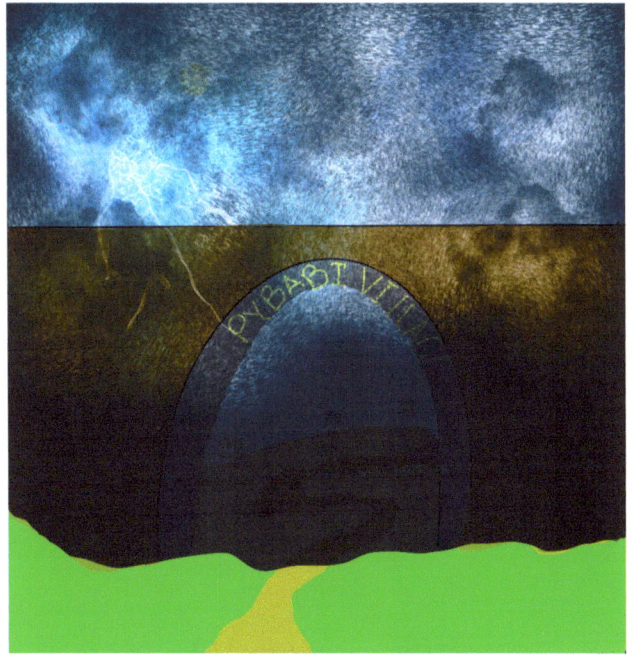

After the storm you may hear people sigh and cry but please remember, that love cannot die.

Balii Banana

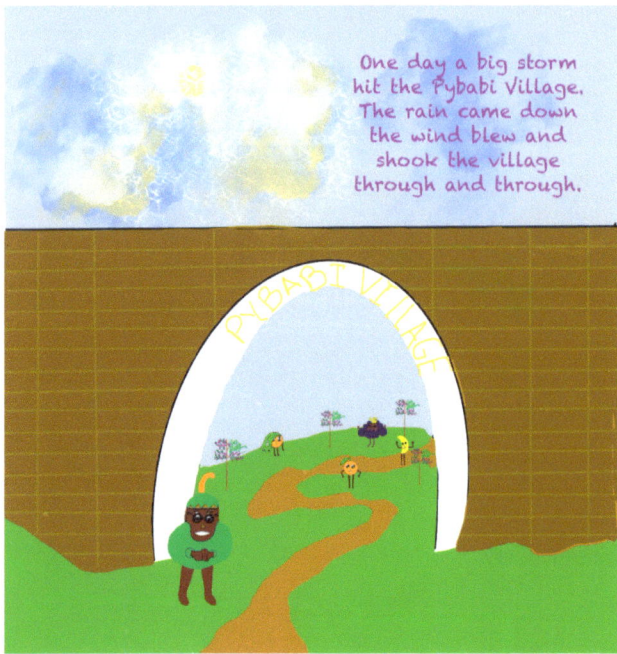

One day a big storm hit the Pybabi Village. The rain came down the wind blew and shook the village through and through.

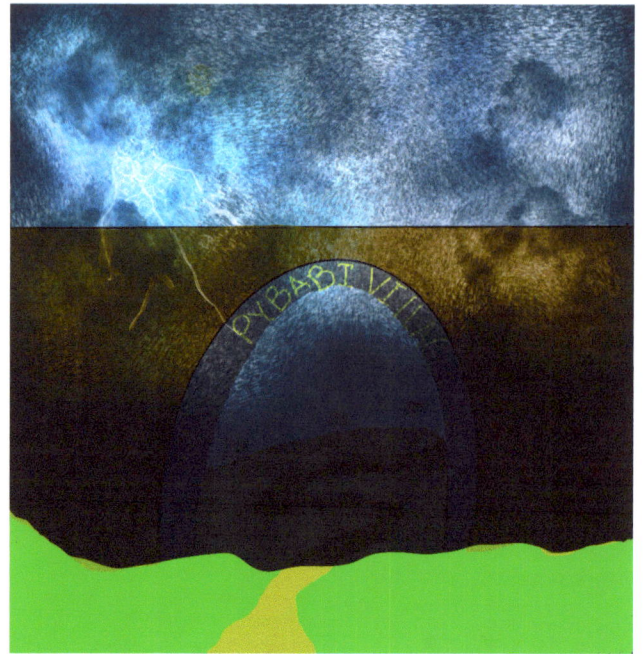

After the storm you may shed a tear but we are glad that you are here.

Lary Berry

7

One day a big storm hit the Pybabi Village. The rain came down the wind blew and shook the village through and through.

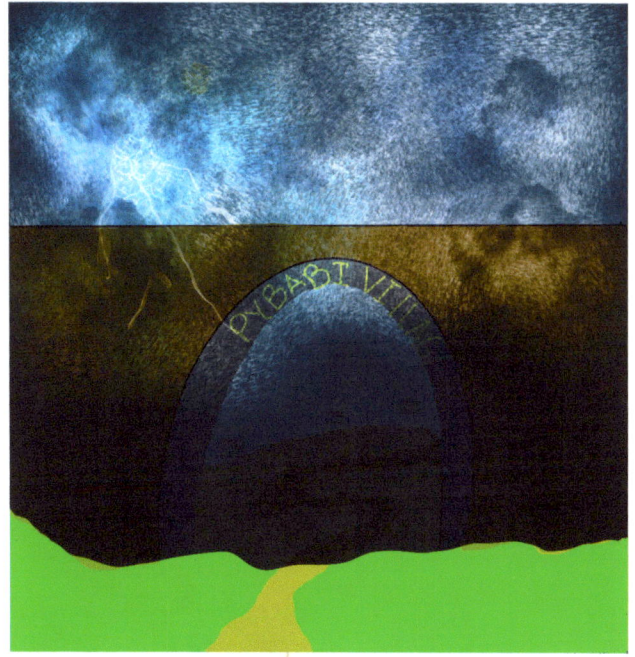

Irene Tangerine

After the storm you may shake like a leaf but the storm can bite no more because it has no teeth.

One day a big storm hit the Pybabi Village. The rain came down the wind blew and shook the village through and through.

After the storm we are left with a big cost but because you are alive all is not lost.

One day a big storm hit the Pybabi Village. The rain came down the wind blew and shook the village through and through.

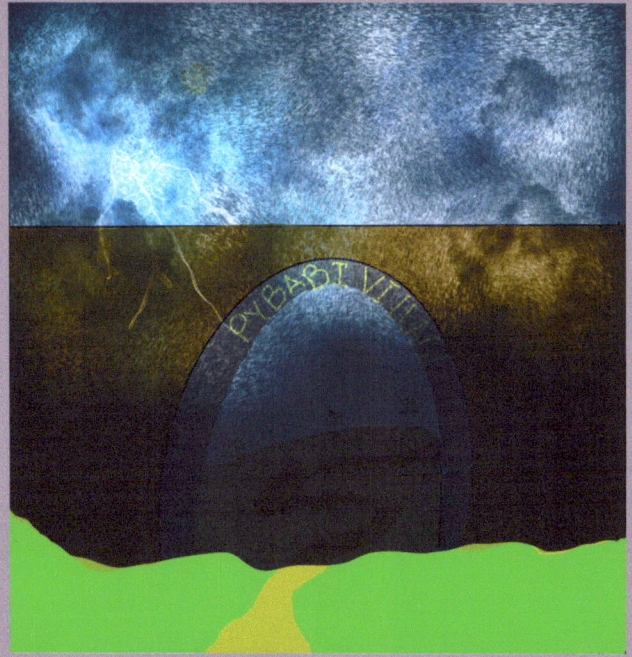

After the storm scared you may feel but the love of good people is very real.

One day a big storm hit the Pybabi Village. The rain came down the wind blew and shook the village through and through.

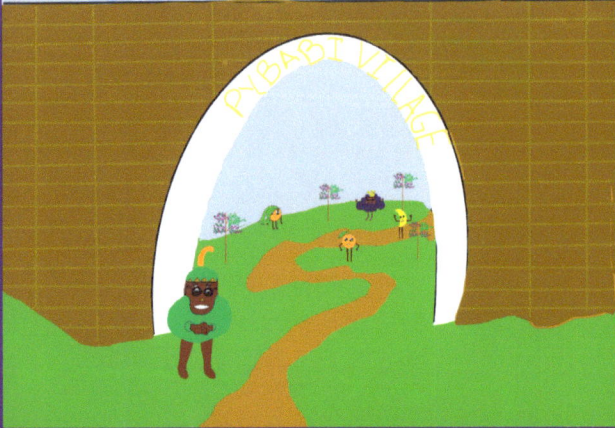

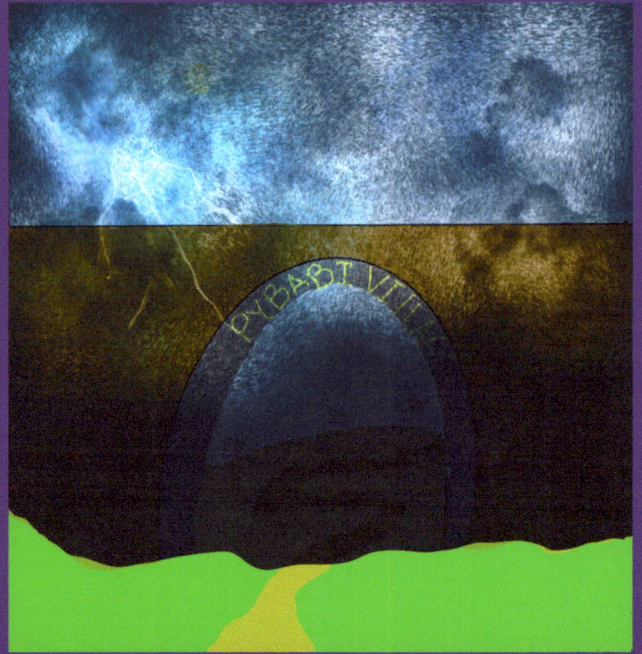

After the storm your loved ones may not have survived but you are here to keep their story alive.

11

One day a big storm
hit the Pybabi Village.
The rain came down
the wind blew and
shook the village
through and through.

After the storm hunger you
may feel but a kind person
will give you a meal.

12

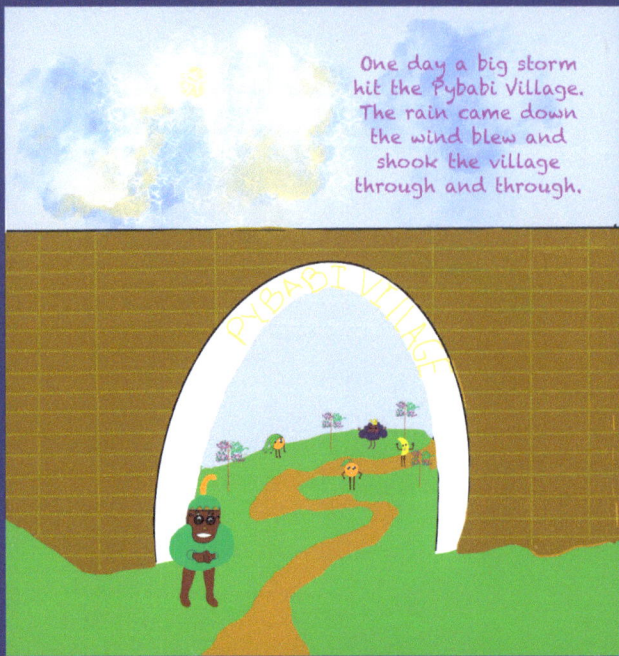

One day a big storm hit the Pybabi Village. The rain came down the wind blew and shook the village through and through.

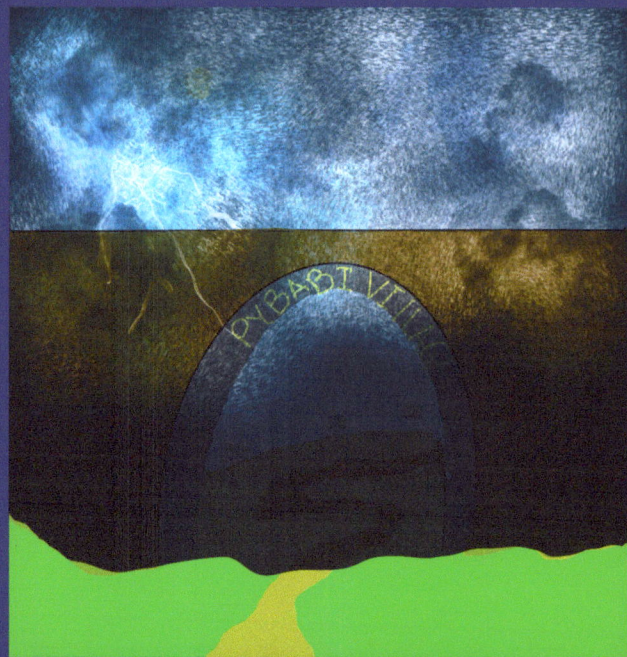

After the storm you look for your stuff but then you smile because your life is enough.

13

One day a big storm hit the Pybabi Village. The rain came down the wind blew and shook the village through and through.

After the storm you may feel you were knocked about but the doctor is coming to check you out.

14

One day a big storm hit the Pybabi Village. The rain came down the wind blew and shook the village through and through.

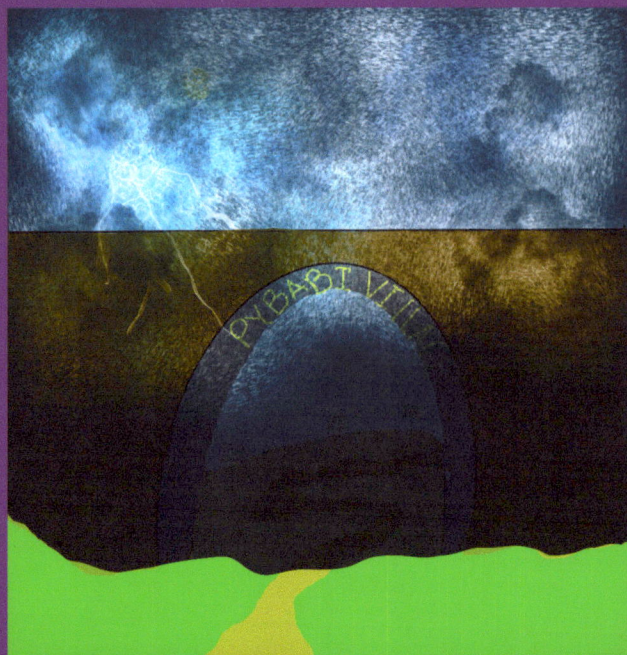

After the storm your clothes may be torn but a kind stranger will wrap you up in something warm.

One day a big storm
hit the Pybabi Village.
The rain came down
the wind blew and
shook the village
through and through.

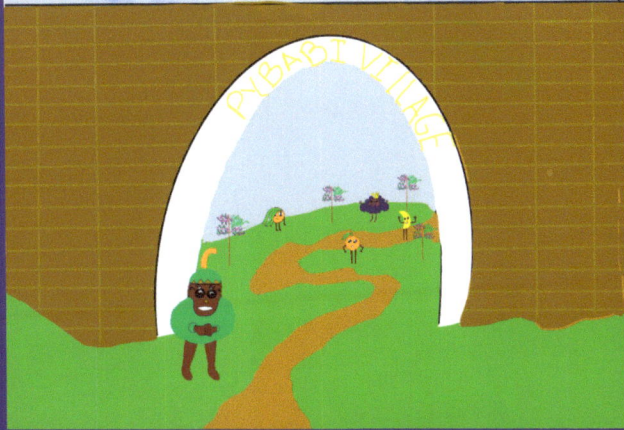

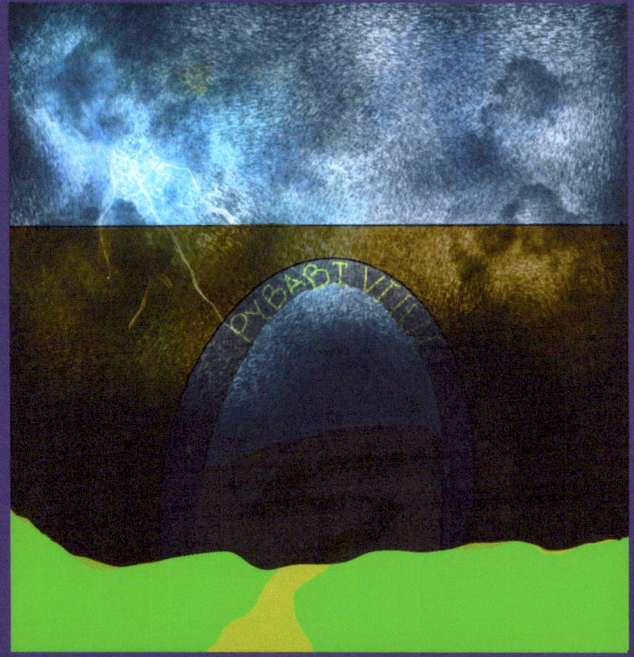

After the storm your heart
may race but the kindness
of mankind will make you
feel safe.

16

One day a big storm hit the Pybabi Village. The rain came down the wind blew and shook the village through and through.

After the storm you may not want to talk but that's ok just ask and we can go on a walk.

17

One day a big storm hit the Pybabi Village. The rain came down the wind blew and shook the village through and through.

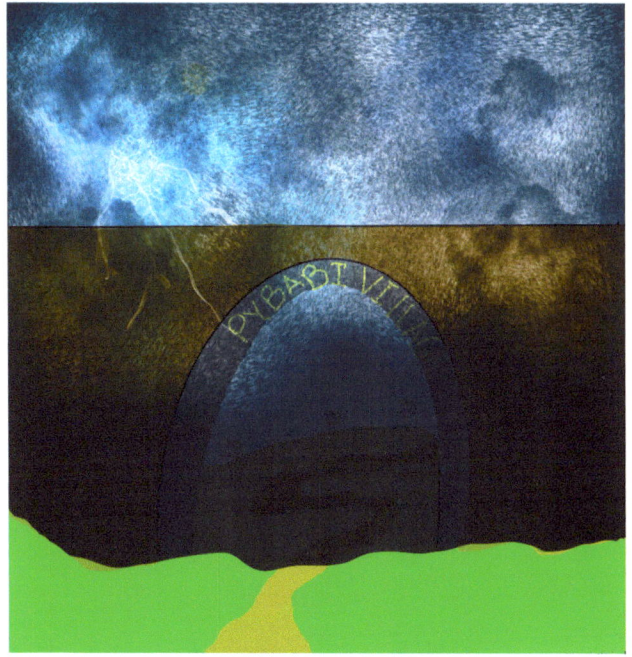

After the storm your tears may be dry but do not worry if the way you truly feel is not seen in your eyes.

18

One day a big storm hit the Pybabi Village. The rain came down the wind blew and shook the village through and through.

After the storm your emotions may be dead but don't feel forced to cry be patient instead.

19

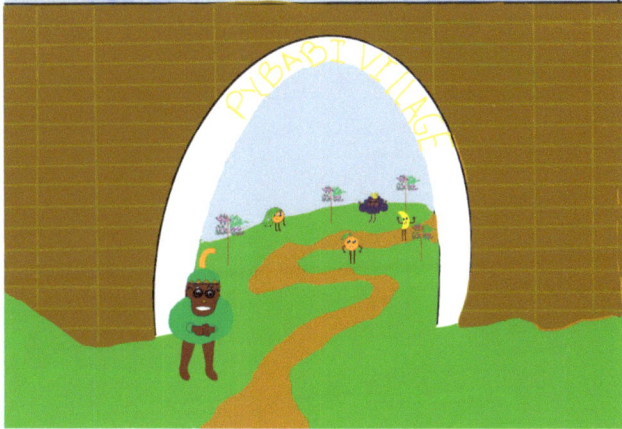

One day a big storm hit the Pybabi Village. The rain came down the wind blew and shook the village through and through.

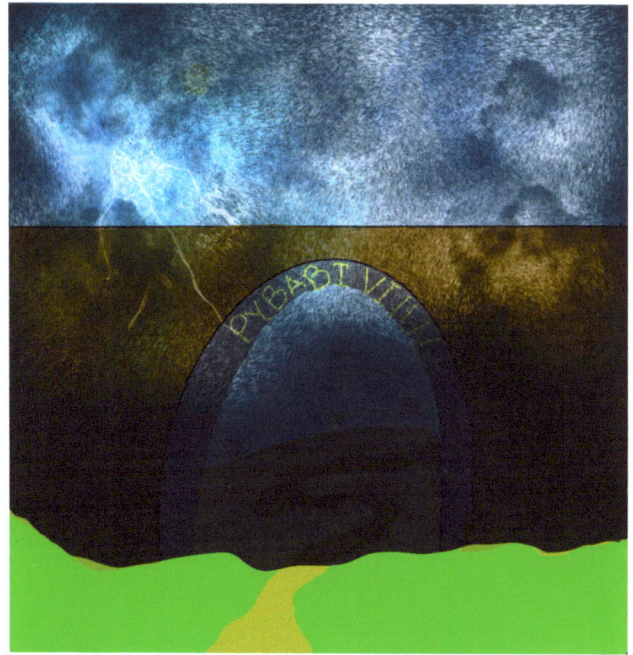

After the storm the loss of someone you love can make you feel depressed but it may help to know that they are in no harm so don't stay awake because they would want you to get some rest.

Disty

One day a big storm hit the Pybabi Village. The rain came down the wind blew and shook the village through and through.

After the storm your thinking is mean but do not worry your thoughts can be cleaned.

Secky

21

One day a big storm hit the Pybabi Village. The rain came down the wind blew and shook the village through and through.

After the storm hate may come up in your heart but you can send it packing by reflecting on the new start.

Any changing property

Any changing property ACP

One day a big storm hit the Pybabi Village. The rain came down the wind blew and shook the village through and through.

SR Star

After the storm your house is no more but do not worry someone will open their door.

23

After the storm you can start a new path but remember you are a pybabi, so don't forget about your math.

PYBABI VILLAGE

For more themes
go to pybabi.com

Can you share your story?

Tiktok @ogi.orange

Twitter @ogi_orange

Instagram @ogi.orange

Email: ogiorange@pybabi.com

www.ingramcontent.com/pod-product-compliance
Lightning Source LLC
Chambersburg PA
CBHW041557040426
42447CB00002B/203